NAUTICAL
knits

12 HANDKNIT DESIGNS

quail studio

photographer jarek duk
stylist georgina brant
hair & make up michelle court
design layout quail studio
model elvira bakteman

First published in Great Britain in 2020 by
Quail Publishing Limited
Old Town Hall, Market Square, Buckingham, Buckinghamshire, MK18 1NJ
E-mail: info@quailstudio.co.uk

ISBN 978-1-9162445-1-1

CONTENTS

12 handknit designs

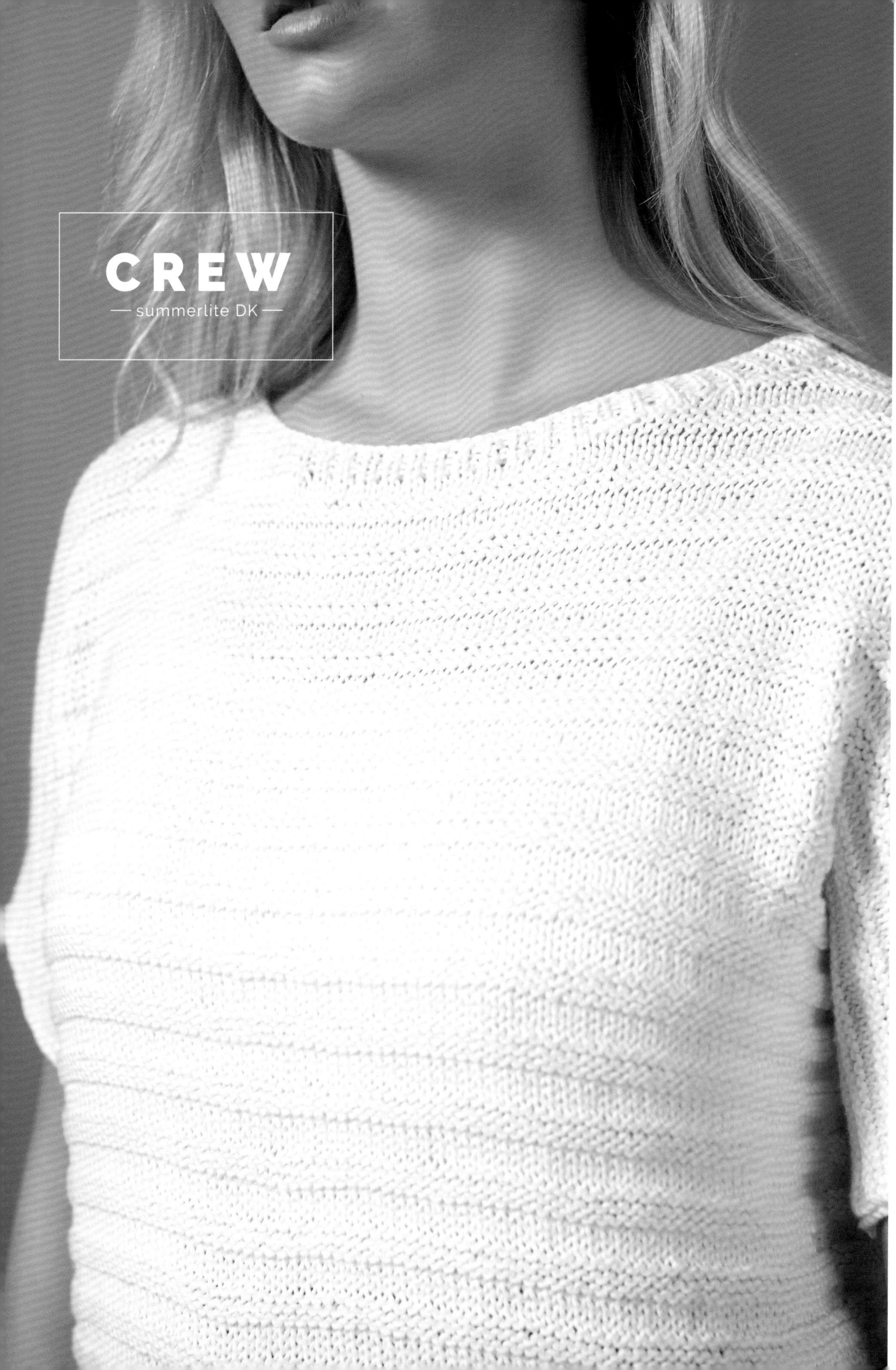
CREW
summerlite DK

FRENCH
— denim revive —

ALPINE
— handknit cotton —

NORTH
— cotton cashmere —

HITCH
— denim revive —

CLOVE
— handknit cotton —

MARINE
— handknit cotton —

BOWLINE
— cotton cashmere —

SLIP
—summerlite DK—

CREW

quail studio

SIZES

To fit bust	81 – 86	91 – 97	102 – 107	112 – 117	122 – 127	cm
	32 – 34	36 – 38	40 – 42	44 – 46	48 – 50	in
Actual Size	95	106	116	125	136	cm
	37 ½	41¾	45½	49	53½	in

YARN

Rowan Summerlite DK (photographed in White 465)

	7	8	8	9	9	x50g

NEEDLES

3¼mm (no 10) (US 3) needles
3¾mm (no 9) (US 5) needles

TENSION

23 stitches and 40 rows to 10cm/4in measured over pattern using 3¾mm (US 5) needles

EXTRAS

Stitch Holders
Stitch Marker

BACK
Using 3¼mm (US 3) needles cast on
110(122,134,144,156) sts.
Row 1: * K1, P1, rep from * to end.
Row 1 forms rib.
Work in rib until back meas 2cm, ending with a WS row.

Change to 3¾mm (US 5) needles.
Row 1: Knit.
Row 2: Purl.
Row 3: Knit.
Rows 1 to 3 form pattern.
Work in pattern until back meas 33(34,35,36,37) cm, ending with a WS row.

Shape for sleeves

Keeping pattern correct, cast on 10 sts at beg of next 4 rows. 150(162,174,184,196) sts.

Place marker at centre of last row.

Work in pattern until back meas 17(18,19,20,21) cm from marker, ending with a WS row.

Shape shoulders

Cast off 10(11,12,13,14) sts at beg of next 10 rows. 50(52,54,54,56) sts.
Leave rem sts on a stitch holder

FRONT
Using 3¼mm (US 3) needles cast on
110(122,134,144,156) sts.
Row 1: * K1, P1, rep from * to end.
Row 1 forms rib.
Work in rib until front meas 2cm, ending with a WS row.

Change to 3¾ mm (US 5) needles.
Row 1: Knit.
Row 2: Purl.
Row 3: Knit.
Rows 1 to 3 form pattern.
Work in pattern until front meas 33(34,35,36,37) cm, ending with a WS row.

Shape for sleeves

Keeping pattern correct, cast on 10 sts at beg of next 4 rows. 150(162,174,184,196) sts.

Work in pattern until front meas 10 rows less than length of back to start of shoulder shaping.

Shape neck

Next Row (RS): Patt 65(70,75,80,85) sts, turn and work on these sts only.
Cast off 3 sts at beg of next and foll 4 alt rows. 50(55,60,65,70) sts.

Shape shoulder

Cast off 10(11,12,13,14) sts at beg of next and foll 3 alt rows. 10(11,12,13,14) sts.
Pattern 1 row.
Cast off.

With RS facing, slip centre 20(22,24,24,26) sts onto a stitch holder, rejoin yarn to rem sts and patt to end. 65(70,75,80,85) sts.

Shape neck
Next Row (WS): Patt to end.
Cast off 3 sts at beg of next and foll 4 alt rows. 50(55,60,65,70) sts.

Shape shoulder

Cast off 10(11,12,13,14) sts at beg of next and foll 3 alt rows. 10(11,12,13,14) sts.
Pattern 1 row.
Cast off.

MAKING UP
Press as described on the information page.
Join right shoulder seam using mattress stitch.

Neckband
With right side facing and using 3¼mm (US 3) needles, pick up and knit 21 sts down left front neck, knit 20(22,24,24,26) sts from front neck stitch holder, pick up and knit 21sts up right front neck, knit 50(52,54,54,56) sts from back neck stitch holder. 112(116,120,120,124) sts.
Row 1: * K1, P1, rep from * to end.
Row 1 forms rib.
Rep row 1, 4 times more.
Cast off in rib.

Join left shoulder and neckband seam.
Join side and underarm seams.

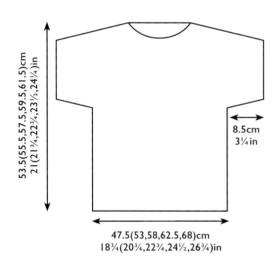

53.5(55.5,57.5,59.5,61.5)cm
21(21¾,22¾,23½,24¼)in

8.5cm
3¼in

47.5(53,58,62.5,68)cm
18¾(20¾,22¾,24½,26¾)in

HALTER

quail studio

SIZES

To fit bust	81 – 86	91 – 97	102 – 107	112 – 117	122 – 127	cm
	32 – 34	36 – 38	40 – 42	44 – 46	48 – 50	in
Actual Size	85	96	107	116	127	cm
	33½	37¾	42¼	45¾	50	in

YARN

Rowan Summerlite DK
A – White 465

	7	7	8	8	9	x 50g

B – Blue 470

	1	1	1	1	1	x 50g

NEEDLES

3¼mm (no 10) (US 3) needles
3¾mm (no 9) (US 5) needles

TENSION

22 stitches and 30 rows to 10cm/4in measured over st st using 3¾mm (US 5) needles

EXTRAS

Stitch Holders

BACK

Using 3¼mm (US 3) needles and yarn B cast on 94(106,118,128,140) sts.
Row 1: * K1, P1, rep from * to end.
Row 1 forms rib.
Using yarn B, work 1 row in rib.

Using yarn A, work 2 rows in rib.
Using yarn B, work 2 rows in rib.
Rep last 4 rows once more.

Change to 3¾mm (US 5) needles.
Work stripe pattern as follows:
Row 1 (RS): Using yarn A, K to end.
Row 2: Using yarn A, P to end.
Rows 3 to 18: Rep rows 1 and 2, 8 times.
Row 19: Using yarn B, K to end.
Row 20: Using yarn B, P to end.
Rows 1 to 20 form stripe pattern.

Work in stripe pattern until back meas 35(35,36,36,36) cm, ending with a WS row.

Shape armholes

Cast off 4 sts at beg of next 2 rows. 86(98,110,120,132) sts.
Row 1: K2, Sl 1, K1, psso, patt to last 4 sts, K2tog, K2.
Row 2: P2, P2tog, patt to last 4 sts, P2tog tbl, P2.
Row 3: K2, Sl 1, K1, psso, patt to last 4 sts, K2tog, K2.
Row 4: Patt to end.
Rep rows 3 and 4 once more, then work row 3 again. 76(88,100,110,122) sts.
Cont straight until armhole meas 18(19,19,20,21) cm, ending on a WS row.

Shape neck

Next Row: Patt 19(24,30,34,39) sts, turn and work on these sts only.
Next Row: P2, P2tog, patt to end. 18(23,29,33,38) sts.
Cast off.

With RS facing slip centre 38(40,40,42,44) sts onto a stitch holder, rejoin yarn to rem sts and patt to end. 19(24,30,34,39) sts.
Next Row: Patt to last 4 sts, P2tog tbl, P2. 18(23,29,33,38) sts.
Cast off.

FRONT

Work as for back to until front meas 18 rows less than length of back to shoulder.

Shape neck

Next Row (RS): Patt 29(35,41,46,52), K2tog, K2, turn and work on these sts only.
32(38,44,49,55) sts.

Row 1: P2, P2tog, patt to end.
Row 2: Patt to last 4 sts, K2tog, K2.
Rep rows 1 and 2, 6(6,6,7,7) times more, then work row 1, 0(1,1,0,1) time.
18(23,29,33,38) sts.
Patt 3(2,2,1,0) rows.
Cast off.

With RS facing slip centre 10 sts onto a stitch holder, rejoin yarn to rem sts, K2, Sl1, K1, psso, patt to end.
32(38,44,49,55) sts.

Row 1: Patt to last 4 sts, P2tog tbl, P2.
Row 2: K2, SL1, K1, psso, patt to end.
Rep rows 1 and 2, 6(6,6,7,7) times more, then work row 1, 0(1,1,0,1) time.
18(23,29,33,38) sts.
Patt 3(2,2,1,0) rows.
Cast off.

SLEEVES (both alike)
Using 3¼mm (US 3) needles and yarn B cast on 50(52,54,54,56) sts.
Row 1: * K1, P1, rep from * to end.
Row 1 forms rib.
Using yarn B, work 1 row in rib.

Using yarn A, work 2 rows in rib.
Using yarn B, work 2 rows in rib.
Rep last 4 rows once more.

Change to 3¾mm (US 5) needles.
Working in stripe pattern as given for back, cont as follows:
Patt 8 rows.
Next Row (RS): K2, M1, patt to last 2 sts, M1, K2.
Patt 5 rows.
Working inc as set above, inc 1 st at each end of next and 1(6,6,8,11) foll 6th rows, then on every foll 8th row to 78(84,86,88,92) sts.

Cont without shaping until sleeve meas 47(48,49,50,51) cm, ending with a WS row.

Shape top
Cast off 4 sts at beg of next 2 rows.
70(76,78,80,84) sts.

Row 1 (RS): K2, Sl 1, K1, psso, patt to last 4 sts, K2tog, K2.
Row 2: P2, P2tog, patt to last 4 sts, P2tog tbl, P2.
Row 3: K2, Sl 1, K1, psso, patt to last 4 sts, K2tog, K2.
Row 4: Patt to end.
Rep rows 3 and 4 twice more.
60(66,68,70,74) sts.
Cast off.

MAKING UP
Press as described on the information page.
Join right shoulder seam using mattress stitch.
Neckband
Using RS facing, using 3¼mm needles and yarn B, pick up and knit 16 sts down left front neck, knit 10 sts from front neck stitch holder inc 3 sts evenly, pick up and knit 16 sts up right front neck, 2 sts down right back neck, knit 38(40,40,42,44) sts from back neck stitch holder inc 7 sts evenly, pick up and knit 2 sts up left back neck.
94(96,96,98,100) sts.
Row 1: * K1, P1, rep from * to end.
Row 1 forms rib.
Using yarn B, work 1 row in rib.

Using yarn A, work 2 rows in rib.
Using yarn B, work 2 rows in rib.
Cast off in rib.

Join left shoulder and neckband seam.
Sew in sleeves.
Join side and sleeve seams.

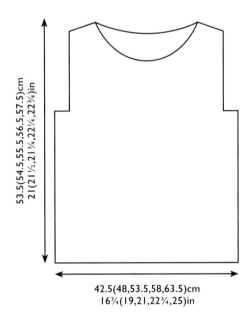

53.5(54.5,55.5,56.5,57.5)cm
21(21½,21¾,22¼,22¾)in

42.5(48,53.5,58,63.5)cm
16¾(19,21,22¾,25)in

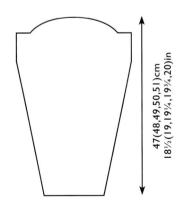

47(48,49,50,51)cm
18½(19,19¼,19¾,20)in

ANCHOR

quail studio

SIZES

To fit bust	81 – 86	91 – 97	102 – 107	112 – 117	122 – 127	cm
	32 – 34	36 – 38	40 – 42	44 – 46	48 – 50	in
Actual Size	108	118	128	138	148	cm
	42½	46½	50½	54¼	58¼	in

YARN

Rowan Handknit Cotton
A – Bleached 263

	10	11	11	12	13	x 50g

B – Turkish Plum 277

	2	2	2	2	2	x 50g

NEEDLES

3¼ mm (no 10) (US 3) needles
4mm (no 8) (US 6) needles
Cable needle

TENSION

20 stitches and 28 rows to 10cm/4in measured over st st using 4mm (US6) needles

EXTRAS

Stitch Holder
Stitch Marker

SPECIAL ABBREVIATIONS

C6B, slip next 3 sts onto cable needle and hold at back, K3, then K3 from cable needle
C6F, slip next 3 sts onto cable needle and hold at front, K3, then K3 from cable needle

BACK

Using 3¼ mm (US 3) needles and yarn B cast on 108(118,126,138,148) sts.
Row 1 (RS): K1(2,2,0,1), * P2, K2, rep from * to last 3(4,4,2,3) sts, P2, K1(2,2,0,1).
Row 2: P1(2,2,0,1), * K2, P2, rep from * to last 3(4, 2,3) sts, K2, P1(2,2,0,1).
Rows 1 and 2 rows form rib.
Using yarn B, work 2 rows in rib.
Using yarn A, work 4 rows in rib.
Using yarn B, work 4 rows in rib and inc 0(0,2,0,0) sts evenly on last row.
108(118,128,138,148) sts.

Change to 4mm (US 6) needles and yarn A
Starting with a K row, work in st st until back meas 40(41,42,43,44) cm, ending with a WS row.

Shape armholes

Cast off 3 sts at beg of next 2 rows.
102(112,122,132,142) sts.
Next Row: K2, Sl 1, K1, psso, K to last 4 sts, K2tog, K2.
Next Row: P2, P2tog, P to last 4 sts, P2tog tbl, P2.
Rep last 2 rows once more. 94(104,114,124,134) sts.

Cont without shaping until armhole meas 19(20,21, 22,23) cm, ending with a WS row.

Shape neck

Next Row: K29(33,37,41,45), turn and work on these sts only.
Next Row: P2, P2tog, P to end. 28(32,36,40,44) sts.

Shape shoulder

Cast off 14(16,18,20,22) sts at beg of next row.
14(16,18,20,22) sts.
P 1 row.
Cast off.

With RS facing slip centre 36(38,40,42,44) sts onto a stitch holder, rejoin yarn to rem sts and K to end. 29(33,37,41,45) sts.

Shape neck

Next Row: P to last 4 sts, P2tog, P2. 28(32,36, 40,44) sts.
K 1 row.

Shape shoulder
Cast off 14(16,18,20,22) sts at beg of next row.
14(16,18,20,22) sts.
K 1 row.
Cast off.

FRONT
Using 3¼ mm (US 3) needles and yarn B cast on
108(118,126,138,148) sts.
Row 1 (RS): K1(2,2,0,1), * P2, K2, rep from * to last
3(4,4,2,3) sts, P2, K1(2,2,0,1).
Row 2: P1(2,2,0,1), * K2, P2, rep from * to last 3(4,4,
2,3) sts, K2, P1(2,2,0,1).
Rows 1 and 2 rows form rib.
Using yarn B, work 2 rows in rib.
Using yarn A, work 4 rows in rib.
Using yarn B, work 4 rows.

Change to 4mm (US 6) needles and yarn A.
Next Row: K25(27,20,32,35), [M1, K24(27,19,32,34)]
1(1,2,1,1) times, P1, (M1, K1) 3 times, P2, (K1, M1)
3 times, P1, [K24(27,19,32,34), M1] 1(1,2,1,1) times,
K25(27,20,32,35).
116(126,136,146,156) sts.
Next Row: P50(55,60,65,70), K1, P6, K2, P6, K1,
P50(55,60,65,70).

Work pattern as follows:
Row 1 (RS): K50(55,60,65,70), P1, K6, P2, K6, P1,
K50(55,60,65,70)
Row 2: P50(55,60,65,70), K1, P6, K2, P6, K1,
P50(55,60,65,70).
Row 3: K50(55,60,65,70), P1, K6, P2, K6, P1,
K50(55,60,65,70)
Row 4: P50(55,60,65,70), K1, P6, K2, P6, K1,
P50(55,60,65,70).
Row 5: K50(55,60,65,70), P1, C6B, P2, C6F, P1,
K50(55,60,65,70).
Row 6: P50(55,60,65,70), K1, P6, K2, P6, K1,
P50(55,60,65,70).
Rows 1 to 6 set cable pattern.
Work in cable pattern until front meas 40(41,42,
43,44) cm, ending with a WS row.

Shape armholes and neck
Next Row (RS): Cast off 3 sts, K45(50,55,60,65)
including st used in casting off, K2tog, P1, patt 6, P1, turn
and work on these 54(59,64,69,74) sts only.

Next Row: K1, patt 6, K1, P to end.
Next Row: K2, Sl 1, K1, psso, K to last 10 sts, K2tog, P1,
patt 6, P1.
Next Row: K1, patt 6, K1, P to last 4 sts, P2tog tbl, P2.
Rep last 2 rows once more. 48(53,58,63,68) sts.

Next Row: K to last 10 sts, K2tog, P1, patt 6, P1.
Next Row: K1, patt 6, K1, P to end.
Rep last 2 rows until 31(35,39,43,47) sts rem.

Cont without shaping until front matches length of back
to start of shoulder shaping, ending with a WS row.

Shape shoulder
Cast off 14(16,18,20,22) sts at beg of next row.
17(19,21,23,25) sts.
Next Row: K1, [P2tog] 3 times, K1, P to end.
14(16,18,20,22) sts.
Cast off.

With RS facing rejoin yarn to rem 58(63,68,73,78) sts
and P1, patt 6, P1, K to end.

Next Row: Cast off 3, P to last 8 sts, K1, patt 6, K1.
Next Row: P1, patt 6, P1, Sl 1, K1, psso, K to last 4 sts,
K2tog, K2.
Next Row: P2, P2tog, P to last 8 sts, K1, patt 6, K1.
Rep last 2 rows once more. 48(53,58,63,68) sts.

Next Row: P1, patt 6, P1, Sl 1, K1, psso, K to end.
Next Row: P to last 8 sts, K1, patt 6, K1.
Rep last 2 rows until 31(35,39,43,47) sts rem.

Cont without shaping until front matches length of back
to start of shoulder shaping, ending with a RS row.

Shape shoulder
Cast off 14(16,18,20,22) sts at beg of next row.
17(19,21,23,25) sts.
Next Row: P1, [p2tog] 3 times, P1, K to end.
14(16,18,20,22) sts.
Cast off.

SLEEVES (both alike)
Using 3¼mm (US 3) needles and yarn B cast on
42(42,46,46,50) sts.
Row 1 (RS): P2(2,0,0,2), * K2, P2, rep from * to last
0(0,2,2,0) sts, K0(0,2,2,0).
Row 2: K2(2,0,0,2), * P2, K2, rep from * to last 0(0,2,
2,0) sts, P0(0,2,2,0).
Rows 1 and 2 rows form rib.
Using yarn B, work 3 rows in rib.
Using yarn A, work 4 rows in rib.
Using yarn B, work 4 rows in rib.

Change to 4mm (US 6) needles and yarn A.
Next Row (RS): K8(8,9,9,10), M1, K8(8,9,9,10), P1,
(M1, K1) 3 times, P2, (K1, M1) 3 times, P1, K8(8,9,9,10),
M1, K8(8,9,9,10). 50(50,54,54,58) sts.
Next Row: P17(17,19,19,21), K1, P6, K2, P6, K1,
P17(17,19,19,21).

Work pattern as follows
Row 1 (RS): K17(17,19,19,21), P1, K6, P2, K6, P1,
K17(17,19,19,21).
Row 2: P17(17,19,19,21), K1, P6, K2, P6, K1,
P17(17,19,19,21).

Row 3: K17(17,19,19,21), P1, K6, P2, K6, P1, K17(17,19,19,21).
Row 4: P17(17,19,19,21), K1, P6, K2, P6, K1, P17(17,19,19,21).
Row 5: K17(17,19,19,21), P1, C6B, P2, C6F, P1, K17(17,19,19,21).
Row 6: P17(17,19,19,21), K1, P6, K2, P6, K1, P17(17,19,19,21).
Rows 1 to 6 set cable pattern.

Working inc sts into cable pattern, inc 1 st at each end of next and every 4th row to 80(82,84,88,92) sts.

Cont without shaping until sleeve meas 35(36,37, 38,39) cm, ending with a WS row.

Shape top
Cast off 3 sts at beg of next 2 rows. 74(76,78,82,86) sts.
Next Row: K2, Sl 1, K1, psso, patt to last 4 sts, K2tog, K2.
Next Row: P2, P2tog, patt to last 4 sts, P2tog tbl, P2.
Rep last 2 rows once more. 66(68,70,74,78) sts.

Next Row: K2, Sl 1, K1, psso, patt to last 4 sts, K2tog, K2. 64(66,68,72,76) sts.
Next Row: Patt to end.
Cast off.

MAKING UP
Press as described on the information page.
Join right shoulder seam using mattress stitch.
Neckband
With RS facing, using 3¼mm (US 3) needles and yarn B, pick up and knit 45(47,49,51,53) sts down left front neck, place marker here, pick up and knit 44(46,48, 50,52) sts up right front neck, 4 sts down right back neck, knit 36(38,40,42,44) sts from back neck stitch holder, inc 1 st at centre, pick up and knit 4 sts up left back neck. 134(140,146,152,158) sts.
Working in stripes of 3 rows in yarn B, 4 rows in yarn A, 4 rows in yarn B, cont as follows
Row 1 (WS): *K2, P2, rep from * to last 2(0,2,0,2) sts, K2(0,2,0,2).
Row 1 set rib.
Row 2: Rib to 3 sts before marker, P2tog tbl, K2, P2tog, rib to end.
Row 3: Rib to 2 sts before marker, K1, P2, K1, rib to end.
Row 4: Rib to 4 sts before marker, K1, Sl 1, K1, psso, K2, K2tog, K1, rib to end.
Row 5: Rib to 3 sts before marker, P6, rib to end.
Row 6: Rib to 3 sts before marker, Sl1, K1, psso, K2, K2tog, rib to end.
Row 7: Rib to 2 sts before marker, P4, rib to end.
Row 8: Rib to 4 sts before marker, P1, P2tog tbl, K2, P2tog, P1, rib to end.
Row 9: Rib to end.
Work row 2 and 3.

Cast off in rib, dec 1 st at each side of K2 sts at centre front as before.

Join left shoulder and neckband seam.
Sew in sleeves.
Join side and sleeve seams.

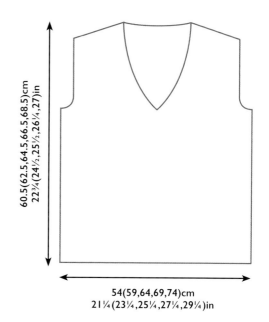

60.5(62.5,64.5,66.5,68.5)cm
22¾(24½,25½,26¼,27)in

54(59,64,69,74)cm
21¼(23¼,25¼,27¼,29¼)in

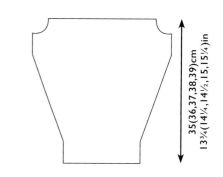

35(36,37,38,39)cm
13¾(14¼,14½,15,15¼)in

36

PEARL

quail studio

SIZES

To fit bust	81 – 86	91 – 97	102 – 107	112 – 117	122 – 127	cm
	32 – 34	36 – 38	40 – 42	44 – 46	48 – 50	in
Actual Size	112	123	132	143	152	cm
	44	48¼	52	56¼	59¾	in

YARN

Rowan Summerlite DK (photographed in White 465)

9	10	11	11	12	x 50g

NEEDLES

3¼mm (no 10) (US 3) needles
3¾mm (no 9) (US 5) needles

TENSION

22 stitches and 30 rows to 10cm/4in measured over stocking stitch using 3¾mm needles

EXTRAS

Stitch Holders

BACK
Using 3¼mm needles cast on 126(138,148,160,170) sts.
Next Row: K1, P1 to end
Last row sets rib.
Work in rib until back meas 6cm, ending with a RS row, dec 1 st at centre of last row. 125(137,147,159,169) sts.

Change to 3¾mm needles.
P 1 row.

Work in patt from chart as folls:

Row 1 (RS): Beg as indicated for your size, work row 1 of chart, working 50-st repeat 2(2, 2, 3, 3) times, end as indicated.
Row 2: P to end.
Row 3: Beg as indicated for your size, work row 3 of chart, working 50-st repeat 2(2, 2, 3, 3) times, end as indicated.
Row 4: P to end.
Rows 5 to 42: Rep last 2 rows 19 times more but working rows 5 to 42 of chart.
Rows 1 to 42 form patt.

Cont in patt until back meas 34 cm.
Mark each end of last row. **

Cont in patt until back meas 18(19,20,21,22) cm from markers, ending with a WS row.

Shape neck
Next Row: Patt 41(46,51,56,61) sts turn and work on these sts only
Next Row: P to end.
Next Row: Patt to last 2sts, K2tog.
Next Row: P to end.
Rep last 2 rows once more. 39(44,49,54,59) sts.
Cast off.

With RS facing, slip next 43(45,45,47,47) sts onto a st holder, rejoin yarn and patt to end. 41(46,51,56,61) sts
Next Row: P to end.
Next Row: K2tog tbl, patt to end.
Next Row: P to end.
Rep last 2 rows once more. 39(44,49,54,59) sts.
Cast off.

FRONT
Work as for back to **.
Cont in patt until front meas 13(14,15,16,16) cm from markers, ending with a WS row.

Shape neck
Next Row (RS): Patt 49(55,60,65,70) sts, turn and work on these sts only.
Next Row: P to end.

Next Row: Patt to last 2 sts, K2tog.
Next Row: P to end.
Rep last 2 rows 9(10,10,10,10) times more.
39(44,49,54,59) sts.

Continue without shaping until front meas same length as back to cast off edge, ending with a WS row.
Cast off.

With RS facing, slip 27(27,27,29,29) sts onto st holder, rejoin yarn and patt to end. 49(55,60,65,70) sts

Next Row: Patt to end.
Next Row: K2tog, patt to end.
Next Row: Patt to end.
Rep last 2 rows 9(10,10,10,10) times more.
39(44,49,54,59) sts.

Continue without shaping unit front meas same length as back to cast off edge, ending with a WS row.
Cast off.

SLEEVES (both alike)
Using 3¼mm needles cast on 52(60,64,68,72) sts.
Next Row: * K1, P1, rep from * to end
Last row sets rib.
Work in rib until sleeve meas 6cm, ending with a RS row, dec 1 st at centre of last row. 51(59,63,67,71) sts.

Change to 3¾mm needles.
P 1 row.

Work in patt from chart as folls:
Row 1 (RS): Beg as indicated for your size, work row 1 of chart, end as indicated.
Row 2: P to end.
Row 3: Beg as indicated for your size, work row 3 of chart, end as indicated.
Row 4: P to end.
Rows 1 to 4 set position of patt.
Taking inc sts into patt, inc 1 st at each end of next and every foll 4th row to 87(93,97,101,105) sts.
Cont without shaping until sleeve meas 31(32,33, 34,35) cm, ending with a WS row.
Cast off.

MAKING UP
Press as described on the information page.
Join right shoulder seam using mattress stitch.
Neckband
With RS facing and using 3¼mm needles, pick up and K20(20,20,20,22) sts down left front neck, K27(27,27,29,29) sts from front neck st holder, pick up and K20(20,20,20,22) sts up right front neck, 5 sts down right back neck, K43(45,45,47,47) sts from back neck st holder, pick up and K5 sts up left back neck.
120(122,122,126,130) sts.
Next Row: * K1, P1, rep from * to end
Last row sets rib.
Work in rib until neckband meas 4cm, ending with a WS row.
Cast off in rib.

Join left shoulder and neckband seam.
Sew on sleeves between markers on back and front.
Join side and sleeve seams.

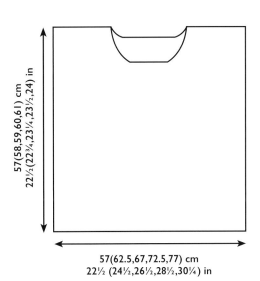

57(58,59,60,61) cm
22½(22¼,23¼,23½,24) in

57(62.5,67,72.5,77) cm
22½ (24½,26½,28½,30¼) in

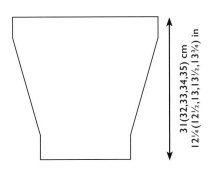

31(32,33,34,35) cm
12¼(12½,13,13½,13¾) in

STITCH KEY

☐	K on RS, P on WS
⊡	Yarn Over (yo)
⊠	Ssk
⊠	K2tog
⊠	K3tog

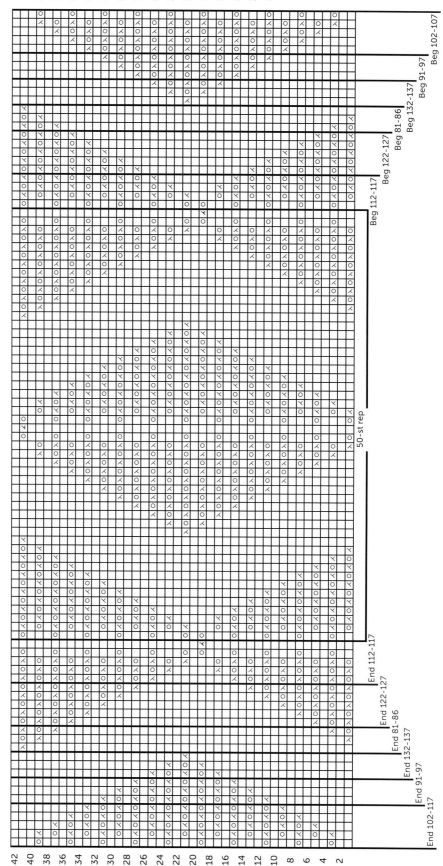

BACK/FRONT CHART

SLEEVE CHART

FRENCH

quail studio

SIZES

To fit bust	81 – 86	91 – 97	102 – 107	112 – 117	122 – 127	cm
	32 – 34	36 – 38	40 – 42	44 – 46	48 – 50	in
Actual Size	96	105	116	125	136	cm
	37¾	41¼	45¾	49¼	53½	in

YARN

Rowan Denim Revive (photographed in Night 213)

	12	14	15	16	18	x 50g

NEEDLES

3¾mm (no 9) (US 5) needles

TENSION

22 stitches and 29 rows to 10cm/4in measured over stocking stitch using 3¾mm needles
24 stitches and 29 rows to 10cm/4in measured over rib using 3¾mm needles

EXTRAS

Cable needle
Stitch Holders

SPECIAL ABBREVIATIONS

C4B – cable 4 back (sl next 2 sts onto cable needle and hold at back of work, K2, then K2 from cable needle)
C4F – cable 4 front (sl next 2 sts onto cable needle and hold at front of work, K2, then K2 from cable needle)

BACK
Using 3¾mm needles cast on 118(128,138,153,163) sts.
Row 1 (RS): P3, * K2, P3, rep from * to end.
Row 2: K3, * P2, K3, rep from * to end.
Last 2 rows set rib.
Work in rib until back meas 59(60,61,62,63)cm, ending with a WS row.

Shape neck

Next Row (RS): Rib 38(43,47,53,57), turn and work on these sts only.
Next Row: Work 2tog, rib to end. 37(42,46,52,56) sts.
Cast off.

With RS facing slip next 42(42,44,47,49) sts onto a st holder, rib to end. 38(43,47,53,57) sts.
Next Row: Rib to last 2 sts, work 2tog. 37(42,46,52,56) sts.
Cast off.

FRONT
Using 3¾mm needles cast on 106(116,128,138,150) sts.
Row 1 (RS): P1, [K2, P3] 7(8,9,10,11) times, C4B, K26(26,28,28,30), C4F, [P3, K2] 7(8,9,10,11) times, P1.
Row 2: K1, [P2, K3] 7(8,9,10,11) times, P34(34,36,36,38), [K3, P2] 7(8,9,10,11) times, K1.
Row 3: P1, [K2, P3] 6(7,8,9,10) times, K2, P1, C4B, K30(30,32,32,34), C4F, P1, K2, [P3, K2] 6(7,8,9,10) times, P1.
Row 4: K1, [P2, K3] 6(7,8,9,10) times, P2, K1, P38(38,40,40,42), K1, P2, [K3, P2] 6(7,8,9,10) times, K1.
Row 5: P1, [K2, P3] 6(7,8,9,10) times, K1, C4B, K34(34,36,36,38), C4F, K1, [P3, K2] 6(7,8,9,10) times, P1.
Row 6: Work the sts as they face.
Row 7: P1, [K2, P3] 5(6,7,8,9) times, K2, P2, C4B, K38(38,40,40,42) sts, C4F, P2, K2, [P3, K2] 5(6,7,8,9) times, P1.
Row 8: Work the sts as they face.

Cont working as set above, working 2 less sts in rib at each side and 4 more sts in st st between cables on centre panel on every right side row until 2(1,2,1,2) rib sts rem at each side.
Next Row: Sl first 2(1,2,1,2) sts onto cable needle and hold at back of work, K2, then K2(1,2,1,2) sts from cable needle, K to last 4(3,4,3,4) sts, sl next 2 sts onto cable needle and hold at front, K2(1,2,1,2), then K2 sts from cable needle.

Starting with a P row, work in st st until front meas 52(53,54,55,56)cm, ending with a WS row.

Shape neck

Next Row (RS): K43(48,52,58,62) sts, turn and work on these sts only.

Next Row: P2, P2tog tbl, P to end.

Next Row: K to end.

Rep last 2 rows 6 times more. 36(41,45,51,55) sts.

Cont without shaping until front matches length of back to shoulder, ending with a WS row.
Cast off.

With RS facing, sl next 20(20,24,22,26) sts onto a st holder, rejoin yarn and K to end. 43(48,51,58,62) sts.

Next Row: P to last 4 sts, P2tog, P2.

Next Row: K to end.

Rep last 2 rows 6 times more. 36(41,45,51,55) sts.

Cont without shaping until front match length of back to shoulder, ending with a RS row.
Cast off.

SLEEVES (both alike)

Using 3¾mm needles cast on 62(62,67,67,72) sts.

Row 1 (RS): K2, * P3, K2, rep from * to end.

Row 2: P2, * K3, P2, rep from * to end.

Last 2 rows set rib.

Working in rib throughout, inc 1 st at each end of foll 5th and every foll 8th row to 86(92,93,95,100) sts.

Cont without shaping until sleeve meas 45(46,47,48,49) cm, ending with a WS row.
Cast off.

MAKING UP

Press as described on the information page.

Join right shoulder seam using mattress stitch.

Neckband

With RS facing and using 3¾mm needles, pick up and K20(20,20,19,19) sts down left front neck, K20(20,24,22,26) sts from front neck st holder, pick up and K19(19,19,19,18) sts up right front neck, 2 sts down right back neck, K42(42,44,47,49) sts from back neck st holder, pick up and K2 sts up left back neck. 105(105,111,111,116) sts.

Row 1: K2(2,3,2,3), * P2, K3, rep from * to last 3(3,3,4,3) sts, P2, K1(1,1.2,1).

Row 2: P1(1,1.2,1), K2, * P3, K2, rep from * to last 2(2,3,2,3) sts, K2(2,3,2,3).

Last 2 rows set rib.

Work in rib until neckband meas 4cm, ending with a WS row.
Cast off in rib.

Join left shoulder and neckband seam.

Place st markers 18(19,20,21,22) cm down from shoulders at side edges of back and front.

Sew in sleeves between markers.

Join side and sleeve seams.

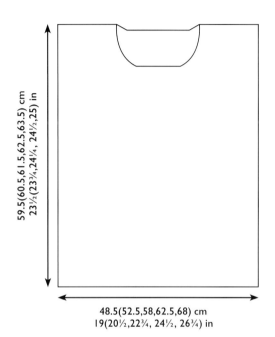

59.5(60.5,61.5,62.5,63.5) cm
23½(23¾,24¼, 24½,25) in

48.5(52.5,58,62.5,68) cm
19(20½,22¾, 24½, 26¾) in

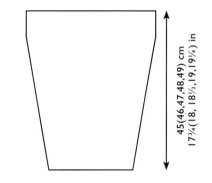

45(46,47,48,49) cm
17¾(18, 18½,19,19¼) in

ALPINE
quail studio

SIZES

To fit bust	81 – 86	91 – 97	102 – 107	112 – 117	122 – 127	cm
	32 – 34	36 – 38	40 – 42	44 – 46	48 – 50	in
Actual Size	96	106	115	126.5	134	cm
	37¾	41¾	45¼	49¾	52¾	in

YARN

Rowan Handknit Cotton (photographed in Bleached)

	13	14	16	17	18	x 50g

NEEDLES

4½mm (no 7) (US 7) needles

TENSION

27.5 sts and 26 rows to 10cm/4in measured over cable pattern using 4.5mm (US 7) needles

EXTRAS

Cable needle
Stitch Holders

BACK

Using 4.5mm (US 7) needles cast on 132 (146, 158, 174, 184) sts.

Beg and ending rows as indicated;
Next row (RS): P1(8,1,9,1), repeat 13 sts from Left Side Chart 2(2,3,3,4) times, work 78 sts from Main Body Chart once, repeat 13 sts from Right Side Chart 2(2,3,3,4) times, P1(8,1,9,1).
Repeating rows 1 – 12 throughout, continue in pattern until back meas 43(44,45,46,47)cm, ending with a WS row.

Shape shoulders and back neck

Cast off 21(24,27,31,33) sts at beg of next 4 rows. 48(50,50,50,52) sts.
Leave rem sts on a stitch holder.

Place stitch marker at each end of row 19(20,21,22,23) cm down from cast off edge. This denotes armholes.

FRONT

Work as for back until front meas 35(36,37,38,39) cm, ending with a WS row.

Shape front neck

Next Row (RS): Patt 52(58,64,72,76), turn.
Next Row: Patt across row.
Next Row: Patt to last 2sts, K2tog. 51(57,63,71,75) sts
Next Row: Patt across row.
Rep last 2 rows to 42(48,54,62,66) sts.
Cont without shaping until front matches length of back to shoulder shaping, ending with a WS row.

Shape shoulders

Cast off 21(24,27,31,33) sts at beg of next and foll alt row.
Fasten off.

With RS facing, slip next 28(30,30,30,32) sts onto a stitch holder, rejoin yarn and pattern to end. 52(58,64,72,76) sts
Next Row (WS): Patt across row.
Next Row: K2tog, patt to end. 51(57,63,71,75) sts
Next Row: Patt across row.
Rep last 2 rows to 42(48,54,62,66) sts.
Cont without shaping until front matches length of back to shoulder shaping, ending with a RS row.

Shape shoulders

Cast off 21(24,27,31,33) sts at beg of next and foll alt row.
Fasten off.

SLEEVES

Using 4.5mm (US 7) needles cast on 58(62,66,70,70) sts.
Row 1 (RS): *K1, P1; rep from * to end.
Last row sets rib.
Work in rib until work meas 8cm, ending with a WS row.

Next Row (RS): P16(18,20,22,22), work 42 sts from sleeve chart once, P16(18,20,22,22).

Repeating rows 1 – 12 throughout, continue in pattern until sleeve meas 47(47,48,49,49)cm, ending with a WS row, AND AT SAME TIME, inc 1 st at each end of foll 3rd and every foll 4th row to 104(108,112,116,120) sts.

Cont without shaping until sleeve meas 47(47,48,49,49) cm, ending with a WS row.

Cast off.

MAKING UP

Press as described on the information page. Join right shoulder with mattress stitch.

Neckband

With RS facing and using 4.5mm (US 7) needles, pick up and knit 20 sts down left front neck, knit 28(30,30,30,32) sts from front neck stitch holder, pick up and knit 20 sts up right front neck, knit 48(50,50,50,52) sts from back neck stitch holder. 116 (120,120,120,124) sts.

Row 1 (WS): K1, P1 to end.

Last row sets rib.

Work in rib until neckband meas 8cm, ending with a WS row.

Cast off in pattern.

Join left shoulder and neckband seams.
Sew in sleeves.
Join side and sleeve seams.

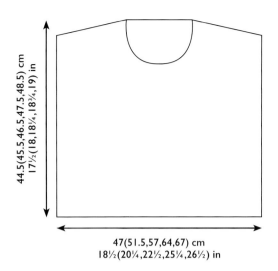

44.5(45.5,46.5,47.5,48.5) cm
17½(18,18¼,18¾,19) in

47(51.5,57,64,67) cm
18½(20¼,22½,25¼,26½) in

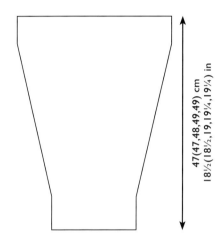

47(47,48,49,49) cm
18½(18½,19,19¼,19¼) in

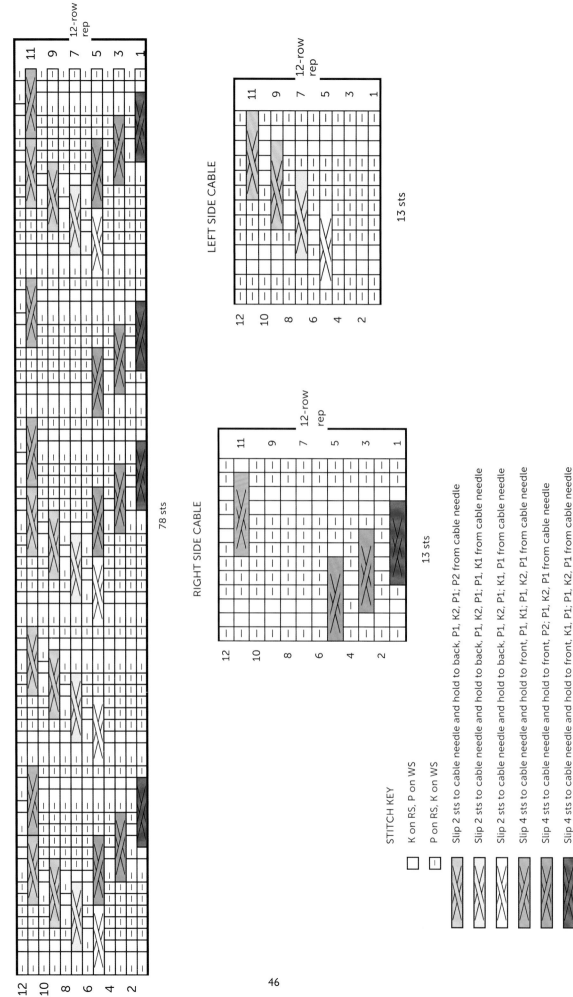

MAIN BODY CABLE

78 sts

12-row rep

LEFT SIDE CABLE

13 sts

12-row rep

RIGHT SIDE CABLE

13 sts

12-row rep

STITCH KEY

☐ K on RS, P on WS

| P on RS, K on WS

Slip 2 sts to cable needle and hold to back, P1, K2, P1; P2 from cable needle

Slip 2 sts to cable needle and hold to back, P1, K2, P1; P1, K1 from cable needle

Slip 2 sts to cable needle and hold to back, P1, K2, P1; K1, P1 from cable needle

Slip 4 sts to cable needle and hold to front, P1, K1; P1, K2, P1 from cable needle

Slip 4 sts to cable needle and hold to front, P2; P1, K2, P1 from cable needle

Slip 4 sts to cable needle and hold to front, K1, P1; P1, K2, P1 from cable needle

NORTH

quail studio

SIZES

To fit bust					
81 – 86	91 – 97	102 – 107	112 – 117	122 – 127	cm
32 – 34	36 – 38	40 – 42	44 – 46	48 – 50	in

Actual Size					
143	154	165	176	187	cm
56¼	60½	63	69¼	73½	in

YARN

Rowan Cotton Cashmere
A – Paper 210

16	16	17	17	18	x 50g

B – Indigo 231

5	5	5	6	6	x 50g

NEEDLES

4½mm (no 7) (US 7) needles

TENSION

18 stitches and 32 rows to 10cm/4in measured over pattern using 4½mm needles and holding 2 strands of yarn together.

EXTRAS

Stitch Holders
Stitch Markers

BACK

Using 4½mm needles and holding 2 strands of yarn A together cast on 131(141,151,161,171) sts.
Work in g st until back meas 4cm, ending with a WS row.

Row 1 (RS): Using yarn A, K to end.
Row 2: Using yarn A, P to end.
Row 3: Using yarn A, K1, * sl 1 purlwise, K1, rep from * to end.
Row 4: Using yarn A, K1, * yf, sl 1 purlwise, yb, K1, rep from * to end.
Rows 5 to 12: Rep rows 1 to 4, twice.
Rows 13 to 16: Holding 2 strands of yarn B together, work rows 1 to 4.
Rows 1 to 16 form stripe pattern.

Work in stripe patt until back meas 39(38.5,38,37.5,37) cm, ending with a WS row.
Place a st marker at each end of last row.
Cont in patt until 8th stripe in B has been worked, ending with a WS row.

Break off yarn B and cont in patt in yarn A only until back meas 18(19,20,21,22) cm from markers, ending with a WS row.

Shape neck

Next Row (RS): Patt 37(42,47,50,55) sts, turn and work on these sts only.
Next Row: Patt 2, work 2tog tbl, patt to end.
Next Row: Patt to last 4 sts, work 2tog tbl, patt 2.
Next Row: Patt 2, work 2tog tbl, patt to end.
34(39,44,47,52) sts.
Cast off.

Slip centre 57(57,57,61,61) sts onto a st holder, rejoin yarn to rem sts and patt to end.
37(42,47,50,55) sts.

Next Row: Patt to last 4 sts, work 2tog, patt 2.
Next Row: Patt 2, work 2tog, patt to end.
Next Row: Patt to last 4 sts, work 2tog, patt 2.
34(39,44,47,52) sts.
Cast off.

FRONT

Using 4½mm needles and holding 2 strands of yarn A together cast on 131(141,151,161,171) sts.
Work in g st until front meas 4cm, ending with a WS row.

Row 1 (RS): Using yarn A, K to end.
Row 2: Using yarn A, P to end.
Row 3: Using yarn A, K1, * sl 1 purlwise, K1, rep from * to end.
Row 4: Using yarn A, K1, * yf, sl 1 purlwise, yb, K1, rep from * to end.
Rows 5 to 12: Rep rows 1 to 4, twice.

Rows 13 to 16: Holding 2 strands of yarn B together, work rows 1 to 4.
Rows 1 to 16 form stripe patt.

Work in stripe patt until front meas 39(38.5,38,37.5,37) cm, ending with a WS row.
Place a st marker at each end of last row.
Cont in stripe patt until 8th stripe in B has been worked, ending with a WS row.

Break off yarn B and cont in patt in yarn A only until front meas 11(12,13,14,15) cm, ending with a WS row.

Shape neck

Next Row (RS): Patt 56(61,66,69,74) sts, turn and work on these sts only.
Next Row: Cast off 2 sts, patt to end.
Next Row: Patt to end.
Rep last 2 rows 10 times more.
34(39,44,47,52) sts.
Cont straight until front meas same length as back to cast off edge, ending with a WS row.
Cast off.

With RS facing slip centre 19(19,19,23,23) sts onto a st holder, rejoin yarn to rem sts and patt to end.
56(61,66,69,74) sts.

Next Row: Patt to end.
Next Row: Cast off 2 sts, patt to end.
Rep last 2 rows 10 times more. 34(39,44,47,52) sts.
Cont straight until front meas same length as back to cast off edge, ending with a WS row.
Cast off.

SLEEVES
Using 4½mm needles and holding 2 strands of yarn A together cast on 39(39,39,43,43) sts.
Work in g st until work meas 4cm, ending with a WS row.

Working in stripe patt as given for back, work 2 rows.
Inc and work into patt 1 st at each end of next and 0(4,8,8,10) foll 4th rows, then on every foll 6th row to 71(75,79,83,87) sts.

Cont straight in patt until sleeve meas 39.5(40.5,41.5,42.5,43.5)cm, ending with a WS row.
Cast off.

MAKING UP
Press as described on the information page.
Join right shoulder seam using mattress stitch.
Neckband
With RS facing, using 4½mm needles and holding 2 strands of yarn A together, pick up and K20 sts down left front neck, K19(19,19,23,23) sts from front neck st holder, pick up and K20 sts up right front neck, 4 sts down right back neck, K57(57,57,61,61) sts from back neck st holder, pick up and K4 sts up left back neck.
124(124,124,132,132) sts.
Row 1: * K1, P1, repeat from * to end.
Row 1 forms rib.
Rep row 1 until neckband meas 4cm, ending with a WS row.
Cast off in rib.

Join left shoulder and neckband seam.
Sew in sleeve between markers on back and front.
Join side and sleeve seams.

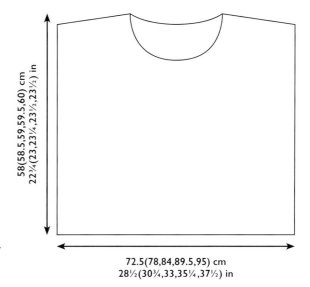

58(58.5,59,59.5,60) cm
22¾(23,23¼,23½,23½) in

72.5(78,84,89.5,95) cm
28½(30¾,33,35¼,37½) in

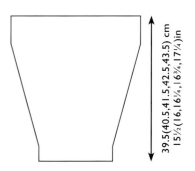

39.5(40.5,41.5,42.5,43.5) cm
15½(16,16¼,16¾,17¼)in

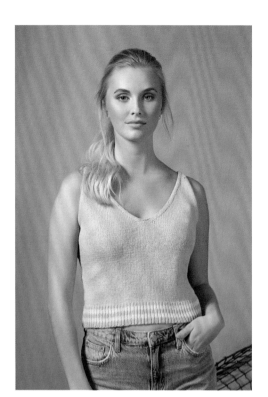

HITCH
quail studio

SIZES

To fit bust	81 – 86	91 – 97	102 – 107	112 – 117	122 – 127	cm
	32 – 34	36 – 38	40 – 42	44 – 46	48 – 50	in
Actual Size	94	105	114	125	134	cm
	37	41¼	45	49¼	52¾	in

YARN

Rowan Denim Revive
A – Bluewash 211

	4	4	5	5	6	x 50g

B – Cream 210

	1	1	1	1	1	x 50g

NEEDLES

2¾mm (no 12) (US 2) needles
3mm (no 11) (US 3) needles

TENSION

22 stitches and 29 rows to 10cm/4in measured over stocking stitch using 3mm needles

EXTRAS

Stitch Markers

BACK AND FRONT (both alike)
Using 2¾mm needles and yarn A, cast on 94(106,116,128,138) sts.
Row 1: * K1, P1, rep from * to end.
Last row sets rib.
Work in rib for a further 3 rows.
Change to yarn B and work 4 rows in rib.
Change to yarn A and work 4 rows in rib.
Change to yarn B and work 4 rows in rib.
Change to yarn A and work 4 rows in rib.

Change to 3mm needles.
Continue with yarn A only.
Starting with a K row, work in st st for 4 rows.

Next Row (RS): K2, M1, K to last 2 sts, M1, K2.

Cont in st st and inc 1 st at each end as set above on every foll 10th row to 106(118,128,140,150) sts.

Cont without shaping until work meas 30(31,32,33,34) cm, ending with a WS row.
Place a st marker at each end of last row.

Shape armholes and neck

Next Row (RS): K2, Sl1, K1, psso, K45(51,56,62,67), K2tog, K2, turn and work on these 51(57,62,68,73) sts only.

2nd, 3rd, 4th and 5th sizes only

Next Row: P to end.
Next Row: K2, Sl1, K1, psso, K to last 4 sts, K2tog, K2.
Rep last 2 rows (6,6,11,11) times more. (43,48,44,49) sts.

All sizes

Next Row: P to end.
Next Row: K to last 4 sts, K2tog, K2.
Next Row: P to end.
Next Row: K2, Sl1, K1, psso, K to last 4 sts, K2tog, K2.
Rep last 4 rows 14(11,12,10,11) times more. 6(7,9,11,13) sts.

Next Row: P to end.
Cast off.

With RS facing, rejoin yarn to rem sts and K2, Sl 1, K1, psso, K to last 4 sts, K2tog, K2.
51(57,62,68,73) sts.

2nd, 3rd, 4th and 5th sizes only

Next Row: P to end.
Next Row: K2, Sl1, K1, psso, K to last 4 sts, K2tog, K2.
Rep last 2 rows (6,6,11,11) times more. (43,48,44,49) sts.

All sizes
Next Row: P to end.
Next Row: K2, Sl1, K1, psso, K to end.
Next Row: P to end.
Next Row: K2, Sl1, K1, psso, K to last 4 sts, K2tog, K2.
Rep last 4 rows 14(11,12,10,11) times more. 6(7,9,11,13) sts.

Next Row: P to end.
Cast off.

MAKING UP
Press as described on the information page.
Join right shoulder seam using mattress stitch.
Neckband
With RS facing, using 2¾mm needles and yarn A, pick
up and K48(50,54,56,60) sts down left front neck,
48(50,54,56,60) sts up right front neck, 48(50,54,56,60) sts
down right back neck and 48(50,54,56,60) sts up left back
neck. 192(200,216,224,240) sts.
Cast off.
Join left shoulder and neckband seam.
Armbands
With RS facing, using 2¾mm needles and yarn A, pick up
and K103(107,111,115,121) sts between st markers.
Cast off.
Work the same for other armhole.
Join side and armband seams.

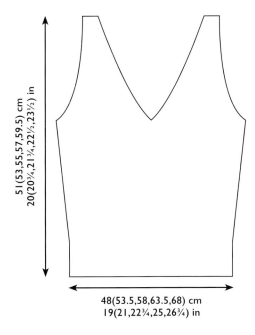

51(53,55,57,59.5) cm
20(20¾,21¾,22¼,23½) in

48(53.5,58,63.5,68) cm
19(21,22¾,25,26¾) in

CLOVE
quail studio

SIZES

To fit bust	81 – 86	91 – 97	102 – 107	112 – 117	122 – 127	cm
	32 – 34	36 – 38	40 – 42	44 – 46	48 – 50	in
Actual Size	96	106	116	126	136	cm
	37¾	41¾	45½	49½	53½	in

YARN

Rowan Handknit Cotton (photographed in Bleached 263)

	10	11	12	13	14	x 50g

NEEDLES

4½mm (no 7) (US 7) needles

TENSION

20 stitches and 28 rows to 10cm /4in measured over st st using 4½mm (US 7) needles

EXTRAS

Stitch Holder

BACK
Using 4½mm (US 7) needles cast on 96(106,116,126,136) sts.
Work in g st for 3cm, ending with a WS row.

Starting with a K row, work in st st for 8 rows.
Starting with a P row, work in rev st st for 8 rows.
Last 16 rows form pattern.
Work in pattern until back meas 33(34,35,36,37) cm, ending with a WS row.

Shape armholes

Cast off 6 sts at beg of next 2 rows. 84(94,104,114,124) sts.
Next Row: Patt 2, work 2tog tbl, patt to last 4 sts, work 2tog, patt 2.
Next Row: Patt to end.
Rep last 2 rows 4 times more. 74(84,94,104,114) sts.

Cont without shaping until armhole meas 19(20,21, 22,23) cm, ending with a WS row.

Shape shoulders

Cast off 11(13,15,17,20) sts at beg of next 2 rows and 10(12,15,17,19) sts at beg of foll 2 rows. 32(34,34,36,36) sts.
Leave rem sts on a stitch holder.

LEFT FRONT
Using 4½mm (US 7) needles cast on 48(53,58,63,68) sts.
Work in g st for 3cm, ending with a WS row.

Starting with a K row, work in st st for 8 rows.
Starting with a P row, work in rev st st for 8 rows.
Last 16 rows form pattern.
Work in pattern until front meas 33(34,35,36,37) cm, ending with a WS row.

Shape armhole

Cast off 6 sts at beg of next row. 42(47,52,57,62) sts.
Next Row: Patt to end.
Next Row: Patt 2, work 2tog tbl, patt to end.
Rep last 2 rows 4 times more. 37(42,47,52,57) sts.
Cont in without shaping until armhole meas 12(13,14,15,16) cm ending with a RS row.

Shape neck

Next Row: Cast off 11(11,11,12,12) sts, patt to end. 26(31,36,40,45,50) sts.

Next Row: Patt to last 4 sts, work 2tog, patt 2.
Next Row: Patt to end.

Rep last 2 rows to 21(25,30,34,39) sts.

Cont without shaping until front matches length of back to start of shoulder shaping, ending with a WS row.

Shape shoulder

Cast off 11(13,15,17,20) sts at beg of next row. 10(12,15,17,19) sts.
Patt 1 row.
Cast off .
RIGHT FRONT
Using 4½mm (US 7) needles cast on 48(53,58,63,68) sts.
Work in g st for 3cm, ending with a WS row.
Starting with a K row, work in st st for 8 rows.

Starting with a P row, work in rev st st for 8 rows.
Last 16 rows form pattern.
Work in pattern until front meas 33(34,35,36,37) cm, ending with a RS row.

Shape armhole
Cast off 6 sts at beg of next row. 42(47,52,57,62) sts.
Next Row: Patt 2, work 2tog, patt to end.
Next Row: Patt to end.
Rep last 2 rows 4 times more. 37(42,47,52,57) sts

Cont without shaping until armhole meas 12(13,14, 15,16) cm, ending with a WS row.

Shape neck
Next Row: Cast off 12(12,12,13,13) sts, patt to end. 25(30,35,39,44) sts.

Next Row: Patt to end.
Next Row: Patt 2, work 2tog tbl, patt to end.
Rep last 2 rows to 21(25,30,34,39) sts.

Cont without shaping until front matches length of back to start of shoulder shaping, ending with a RS row.

Shape shoulder
Cast off 11(13,15,17,20) sts at beg of next row. 10(12,15,17,19) sts.
Patt 1 row.
Cast off .

SLEEVES (both alike)
Using 4½mm (US 7) needles cast on 46(50,54,58,62) sts.
Work in g st for 3cm, ending with a WS row.

Starting with a K row, work in st st for 8 rows.
Starting with a P row, work in rev st st for 8 rows.
Last 16 rows form pattern.
Keep pattern correct, inc 1 st at each end of next and every foll 6th row to 76(80,84,88,92) sts.
Cont without shaping until sleeve meas 39(40,41, 42,43) cm, ending with same patt row as back before armhole shaping.

Shape top
Cast off 6 sts at beg of next 2 rows. 64(68,72,76,80) sts.

Next Row: Patt 2, work 2tog tbl, patt to last 4 sts, work 2tog, patt 2.
Next Row: Patt to end.
Rep last 2 rows 4 times more. 54(58,62,66,70) sts.

Next Row: Patt 2, work 2tog tbl, patt to last 4 sts, work 2tog, patt 2.
Next Row: Patt 2, work 2tog, patt to last 4 sts, work 2tog tbl, patt 2.
Rep last 2 rows 4 times more. 34(38,42,46,50) sts.
Cast off.

MAKING UP
Press as described on the information page.
Front bands
With RS facing and using 4½mm (US 7) needles, pick up and knit 110(114,118,124,128) sts up front edge of one front.
Work in g st for 1.5cm, ending with a WS row.
Cast off.
Work other side to match.
Join both shoulder seams using mattress stitch.
Collar
With RS facing and using 4½mm (US 7) needles, pick up and knit 4 sts from right front band, 24 sts up right front neck, knit 32(34,34,36,36) sts from back neck stitch holder, pick up and knit 24 sts down left front neck and 4 sts from left front band. 88(90,90,92,92) sts.
Work in g st for 3cm, ending with a WS row.
Cast off.
Sew in sleeves.
Join side and sleeve seams.

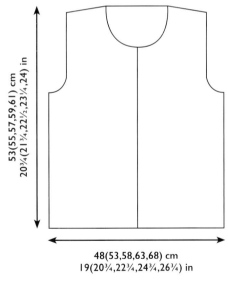

53(55,57,59,61) cm
20¾(21¾,22½,23¾,24) in

48(53,58,63,68) cm
19(20¾,22¾,24¾,26¾) in

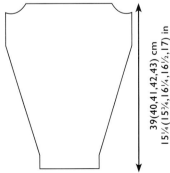

39(40,41,42,43) cm
15¼(15¾,16¼,16½,17) in

MARINE
quail studio

SIZES

To fit bust	81 – 86	91 – 97	102 – 107	112 – 117	122 – 127	cm
	32 – 34	36 – 38	40 – 42	44 – 46	48 – 50	in
Actual Size	95	103	115	123	135	cm
	37½	40½	45¼	48½	53	in

YARN

Rowan Handknit Cotton (photographed in Turkish Plum 277)

	15	16	17	18	19	x 50g

NEEDLES

4½mm (no 7) (US 7) needles
4½mm (no 7) (US 7) circular needle

TENSION

20 stitches and 30 rows to 10cm/4in measured over pattern using 4½mm (US 7) needles

EXTRAS

Stitch Holders

BACK

Using 4½mm needles cast on 95(103,115,123,135) sts.
Row 1 (RS): K3, *P1, K3, rep from * to end.
Row 2: K1, P1, *K3, P1, rep from * to last st, K1.
Last 2 rows set patt.
Work in patt until back meas 46(46,48,48,48) cm, ending with a WS row.

Shape raglan armholes

Cast off 1(2,2,3,3) sts at beg of next 2 rows.
93(99,111,117,129) sts.

3rd, 4th and 5th sizes only

Next Row: Work 2tog, patt to last 2 sts, work 2tog.
Next Row: Work 2tog, patt to last 2 sts, work 2tog.
Next Row: Patt to end.
Rep last 3 rows (5,5,11) times more. (87,93,81) sts.

All sizes

Next Row: Work 2tog, patt to last 2 sts, work 2tog.
Next Row: Patt to end.
Rep last 2 rows 29(31,24,26,19) times more.
33(35,37,39,41) sts.
Leave rem sts on a st holder.

LEFT FRONT

Using 4½mm needles cast on 51(55,63,67,71) sts.
Row 1 (RS): K3, *P1, K3, rep from * to end.
Row 2: K1, P1, * K3, P1, rep from * to last st, K1.
Last 2 rows set patt.
Work in patt until front meas 40 rows less than back to armhole shaping, ending with a WS row.

Shape front

Next Row (RS): Patt to last 2 sts, work 2tog.
Work 5 rows in patt.
Rep last 6 rows, 5 times more.
Next Row: Patt to last 2 sts, work 2 tog.
44(48,56,60,64) sts.
Work 3 rows in patt.

Shape raglan armhole

Cast off 1(2,2,3,3) sts at beg of next row. 43(46,54,57,61) sts.
Work 1 row in patt.

1st and 2nd sizes only

Next Row (RS): Work 2tog, patt to last 2 sts, work 2tog.
Next Row: Patt to end.
Next Row: Work 2tog, patt to end.
Next Row: Patt to end.
Next Row: Work 2tog, patt to end.
Next Row: Patt to end.
Rep last 6 rows twice more. 31(34) sts.

3rd, 4th and 5th sizes only

Next Row: Work 2tog, patt to last 2 sts, work 2tog.

Next Row: Patt to last 2 sts, work 2tog.
Next Row: Patt to end.
Next Row: Patt to last 2 sts, work 2tog.
Next Row: Work 2tog, patt to end.
Next Row: Patt to end.
Rep last 6 rows (2,2,3) times more. (39,42,41) sts.

5th size only
Next Row: Work 2tog, patt to last 2 sts, work 2tog.
Next Row: Patt to last 2 sts, work 2tog.
Next Row: Patt to end.
Next Row: Patt to last 2 sts, work 2tog.
Next Row: Work 2tog, patt to last 2 sts, work 2tog.
Next Row: Patt to end.
Next Row: Work 2tog, patt to end.
Next Row: Patt to last 2 sts, work 2tog.
Next Row: Patt to last 2 sts, work 2tog.
Next Row: Patt to last 2 sts, work 2tog.
Next Row: Work 2tog, patt to end.
Next Row: Patt to end. 30 sts.

All sizes
Next Row: Work 2tog, patt to last 2 sts, work 2tog.
Next Row: Patt to end.
Next Row: Work 2tog, patt to end.
Next Row: Patt to end.
Rep last 4 rows 7(8,11,12,7) times more. 7(7,3,3,6) sts.
Next Row: Work 2tog, patt to end.
Next Row: Patt to end.
Rep last 2 rows 4(4,0,0,3) times more. 2 sts.
Work 2 tog and fasten off.

RIGHT FRONT
Using 4½mm needles cast on 51(55,63,67,71) sts.
Row 1 (RS): K3, *P1, K3, rep from * to end.
Row 2: K1, P1, * K3, P1, rep from * to last st, K1.
Last 2 rows set patt.
Work in patt until front meas 40 rows less than back to armhole shaping, ending with a WS row.

Shape front
Next Row (RS): Work 2tog, patt to end.
Work 5 rows in patt.
Rep last 6 rows, 5 times more.
Next Row: Work 2tog, patt to end.
44(48,56,60,64) sts.
Work 4 rows in patt.

Shape raglan armhole
Cast off 1(2,2,3,3) sts at beg of next row. 43(46,54,57,61) sts.

1st and 2nd sizes only
Next Row (RS): Work 2tog, patt to last 2 sts, work 2tog.
Next Row: Patt to end.
Next Row: Patt to last 2 sts, work 2tog.
Next Row: Patt to end.
Next Row: Patt to last 2 sts, work 2tog.

Next Row: Patt to end.
Rep last 6 rows twice more. 31(34) sts.

3rd, 4th and 5th sizes only
Next Row: Work 2tog, patt to last 2 sts, work 2tog.
Next Row: Work 2tog, patt to end.
Next Row: Patt to end.
Next Row: Work 2tog, patt to end.
Next Row: Patt to last 2 sts, work 2tog.
Next Row: Patt to end.
Rep last 6 rows (2,2,3) times more. (39,42,41) sts.

5th size only
Next Row: Work 2tog, patt to last 2 sts, work 2tog.
Next Row: Work 2tog, patt to end.
Next Row: Patt to end.
Next Row: Work 2tog, patt to end.
Next Row: Work 2tog, patt to last 2 sts, work 2tog.
Next Row: Patt to end.
Next Row: Patt to last 2 sts, work 2tog.
Next Row: Work 2tog, patt to end.
Next Row: Work 2tog, patt to end.
Next Row: Work 2tog, patt to end.
Next Row: Patt to last 2 sts, work 2tog.
Next Row: Patt to end. 30 sts.

All sizes
Next Row: Work 2tog, patt to last 2 sts, work 2tog.
Next Row: Patt to end.
Next Row: Patt to last 2 sts, work 2tog.
Next Row: Patt to end.
Rep last 4 rows 7(8,11,12,7) times more. 7(7,3,3,6) sts.

Next Row: Patt to last 2 sts, work 2tog.
Next Row: Patt to end.
Rep last 2 rows 4(4,0,0,3) times more. 2 sts.
Work 2 tog and fasten off.

SLEEVES (both alike)
Using 4½mm needles cast on 47(47,51,51,55) sts.
Row 1 (RS): K3, *P1, K3, rep from * to end.
Row 2: K1, P1, * K3, P1, rep from * to last st, K1.
Last 2 rows set patt.
Inc and work into patt 1 st at each end of next and 0(4,0,8,6) foll 6th rows, then on every foll 8th row to 73(77,81,85,89) sts.
Cont straight until sleeve meas 44(45,46,47,48) cm, ending with a WS row.

Shape raglan top
Cast off 1(2,2,3,3) sts at beg of next 2 rows.
71(73,77,79,83) sts.

2nd, 3rd, 4th and 5th sizes only
Next Row: Work 2tog, patt to last 2 sts, work 2tog.
Next Row: Patt to end.
Next Row: Patt to end.
Next Row: Patt to end.
Rep last 4 rows (0,0,1,1) time more. (71,75,75,79) sts.

All sizes
Next Row: Work 2tog, patt to last 2 sts, work 2tog.
Next Row: Patt to end.
Rep last 2 rows, 29(29,31,31,33) times more. 11 sts.
Leave rem sts on a st holder.

MAKING UP
Press as described on the information page.
Join all raglan seams using mattress stitch.
Front band
With RS facing and using 4½mm circular needle pick up
and K165(168,174,178,182) sts up right front, K11 sts
from right sleeve st holder, K33(35,37,39,41) sts from
back neck st holder, K11 sts from left sleeve st holder,
pick up and K165(168, 174,178,182) sts down left front.
385(393,407,417,427) sts.
Cast off.

Pockets (make 2)
Using 4½mm needles cast on 43 sts.
Row 1 (RS): K3, * P1, K3, rep from * to end.
Row 2: K1, P1, * K3, P1, rep from * to last st, K1.
Last 2 rows set patt.
Work in patt until pocket meas 15cm, ending with a
WS row.
Cast off.

Join side and sleeve seams.
Attach pockets

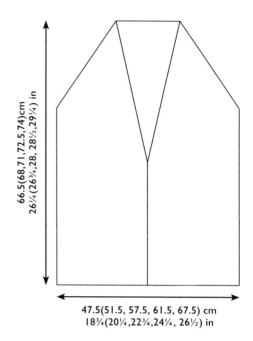

66.5(68,71,72.5,74)cm
26¼(26¾,28, 28½,29¼) in

47.5(51.5, 57.5, 61.5, 67.5) cm
18¾(20¼,22¾,24¼, 26½) in

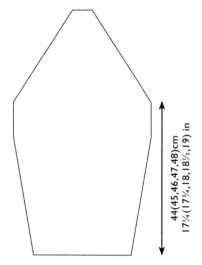

44(45,46,47,48)cm
17¼(17¾,18,18½,19) in

BOWLINE
quail studio

SIZES

To fit bust	81 – 86	91 – 97	102 – 107	112 – 117	122 – 127	cm
	32 – 34	36 – 38	40 – 42	44 – 46	48 – 50	in
Actual Size	92	102	112	122	132	cm
	36¼	40¼	44	48	52	in

YARN

Rowan Cotton Cashmere
A – Paper 210

	6	6	7	7	8	x 50gm

B – Indigo 231

	2	2	2	2	3	x 50gm

NEEDLES

3¼mm (no 10) (US 3) needles
4mm (no 8) (US 6) needles

TENSION

20 stitches and 28 rows to 10cm/4in measured over stocking stitch using 4mm needles

BACK
Using 3¼mm needles and yarn A cast on 92(102,112,122,132) sts.
Row 1: * K1, P1, rep from * to end.
Row 1 forms rib.
Cont in rib until work meas 12cm, ending with a WS row.

Change to 4mm (US 6) needles.

Work in stripe patt as follows:
Row 1 (RS): Using yarn B, K to end.
Row 2: Using yarn B, P to end.
Rows 3 to 6: Rep rows 1 and 2, twice.
Row 7: Using yarn A, K to end.
Row 8: Using yarn A, P to end.
Rows 9 to 34: Rep rows 1 and 2, 13 times.
These 34 rows form stripe patt.

Working in stripe patt throughout, cont until back meas 47(47,48,48,49)cm, ending with a WS row.

Shape armhole
Cast off 4 sts at beg of next 2 rows. 84(94,104,114,124) sts.
Next Row (RS): K2, Sl 1, K1, psso, K to last 4 sts, K2tog, K2.
Next Row: P2, P2tog, P to last 4 sts, P2tog tbl, P2. 80(90,100,110,120) sts.
Next Row: K2, Sl 1, K1, psso, K to last 4 sts, K2tog, K2.

Next Row: P to end.
Rep last 2 rows, 3 times more. 72(82,92,102,112) sts.

Cont straight until armhole meas 18(19,19,20,21) cm, ending with a WS row.

Shape neck
Next Row: K26(30,35,39,44), turn and work on these sts only.
Next Row: P2, P2tog, P to end. 25(29,34,38,43) sts.
Cast off.

With RS facing, rejoin yarn and cast off centre 20(22,22,24,24) sts, patt to end.
26(30,35,39,44) sts.
Next Row: P to last 4 sts, P2tog tbl, P2. 25(29,34,38,43) sts.
Patt 1 row. Cast off.

LEFT FRONT
Using 3¼mm needles and yarn A cast on 52(58,62,68,72) sts.
Row 1: * P1, K1, rep from * to end.
Row 1 forms rib.
Cont in rib until work meas 12cm, ending with a WS row.

Change to 4mm needles.

Work in stripe patt as follows:
Row 1 (RS): Using yarn B, K to last 6 sts, [P1, K1] 3 times.
Row 2: Using yarn B, [P1, K1] 3 times, P to end.
Rows 3 to 6: Rep rows 1 and 2, twice.
Row 7: Using yarn A, K to last 6 sts, [P1, K1] 3 times.

Row 8: Using yarn A, [P1, K1] 3 times, P to end.
Rows 9 to 34: Rep rows 1 and 2, 13 times.
These 34 rows form stripe pattern.

Working in stripe patt throughout, cont until front meas 42 rows less than back to start of armhole shaping, ending with a WS row.

Shape neck
Next Row (RS): K to last 9 sts, K2tog, K1, [P1, K1] 3 times.
Next Row: [P1, K1] 3 times, P to end.
Next Row: K to last 6 sts, [P1, K1] 3 times.
Next Row: [P1, K1] 3 times, P to end.
Next Row: K to last 6 sts, [P1, K1] 3 times.
Next Row: [P1, K1] 3 times, P to end.
Rep last 6 rows, 6 times more. 45(51,55,61,65) sts.

Shape armhole
Next Row: Cast off 4 sts, K to last 9 sts, K2tog, K1, [P1, K1] 3 times. 40(46,50,56,60) sts.
Next Row: [P1, K1] 3 times, P to end.
Next Row: K2, Sl 1, K1, psso, K to last 6 sts, [P1, K1] 3 times.
Next Row: [P1, K1] 3 times, P to last 4 sts, P2tog, P2. 38(44,48,54,58) sts.
Next Row: K2, Sl 1, K1, psso, K to last 6 sts, [P1, K1] 3 times.
Next Row: [P1, K1] 3 times, P to end.
Next Row: K2, Sl 1, K1, psso, K to last 9 sts, K2tog, K1, [P1, K1] 3 times.
Next Row: [P1, K1] 3 times, P to end.
Next Row: K2, Sl 1, K1, psso, K to last 6 sts, [P1, K1] 3 times.
Rep last 2 rows once more. 33(39,43,49,53) sts.
Next Row: [P1, K1] 3 times, P to end.
Next Row: K to last 9 sts, K2tog, K1, [P1, K1] 3 times.
Next Row: [P1, K1] 3 times, P to end.
Next Row: K to last 6 sts, [P1, K1] 3 times.
Next Row: [P1, K1] 3 times, P to end.
Next Row: K to last 6 sts, [P1, K1] 3 times.
Rep last 6 rows 0(2,1,3,2) times more. 32(36,41,45,50) sts.
Next Row: [P1, K1] 3 times, P to end.
Next Row: K to last 9 sts, K2tog, K1, [P1, K1] 3 times. 31(35,40,44,49) sts.
Next Row: [P1, K1] 3 times, P to end.
Next Row: K to last 6 sts, [P1, K1] 3 times.
Rep last 2 rows until front meas same as back to shoulder, ending with a WS row.

Shape shoulder and back neck band
Next row: Cast off 25(29,34,38,43), rib to end. 6 sts.
Cont in rib until band reaches halfway round back neck when slightly stretched, ending with WS row.
Cast off in rib.

RIGHT FRONT
Using 3¼mm needles and yarn A cast on 52(58,62,68,72) sts.
Row 1: * K1, P1, rep from * to end.
Row 1 forms rib.
Cont in rib until work meas 12cm, ending with a WS row.

Change to 4mm needles.

Work in stripe patt as follows:
Row 1 (RS): Using yarn B, [K1, P1] 3 times, K to end.
Row 2: Using yarn B, P to last 6 sts, [K1, P1] 3 times.
Rows 3 to 6: Rep rows 1 and 2, twice.
Row 7: Using yarn A, [K1, P1] 3 times, K to end.
Row 8: Using yarn A, P to last 6 sts, [K1, P1] 3 times.
Rows 9 to 34: Rep rows 1 and 2, 13 times.
These 34 rows form stripe patt.

Working in stripe patt throughout, cont until front meas 42 rows less than back to start of armhole shaping, ending with a WS row.

Shape neck
Next Row (RS): [K1, P1] 3 times, K1, Sl 1, K1, psso, K to end.
Next Row: P to last 6 sts, [K1, P1] 3 times.
Next Row: [K1, P1] 3 times, K to end.
Next Row: P to last 6 sts, [K1, P1] 3 times.
Next Row: [K1, P1] 3 times, K to end.
Next Row: P to last 6 sts, [K1, P1] 3 times.

Rep last 6 rows, 6 times more. 45(51,55,61,65) sts.

Next Row: [K1, P1] 3 times, K1, Sl 1, K1, psso, K to end. 44(50,54,60,64) sts.

Shape armhole
Next Row: Cast off 4 sts, P to last 6 sts, [K1, P1] 3 times. 40(46,50,56,60) sts.
Next Row: [K1, P1] 3 times, K to last 4 sts, K2tog, K2.
Next Row: P2, P2tog, P to last 6 sts, [K1, P1] 3 times. 38(44,48,54,58) sts.
Next Row: [K1, P1] 3 times, K to last 4 sts, K2tog, K2.
Next Row: P to last 6 sts, [K1, P1] 3 times.
Next Row: [K1, P1] 3 times, K1, Sl 1, K1, psso, K to last 4 sts, K2tog, K2.
Next Row: P to last 6 sts, [K1, P1] 3 times.
Next Row: [K1, P1] 3 times, K to last 4 sts, K2tog, K2.
Rep last 2 rows once more. 33(39,43,49,53) sts.
Next Row: P to last 6 sts, [K1, P1] 3 times.
Next Row: [K1, P1] 3 times, K1, Sl 1, K1, psso, K to end.
Next Row: P to last 6 sts, [K1, P1] 3 times.
Next Row: [K1, P1] 3 times, K to end.
Next Row: P to last 6 sts, [K1, P1] 3 times.
Next Row: [K1, P1] 3 times, K to end.
Rep last 6 rows 0(2,1,3,2) times more. 32(36,41,45,50) sts.

Next Row: P to last 6 sts, [K1, P1] 3 times.
Next Row: [K1, P1] 3 times, K1, Sl 1, K1, psso, K to end. 31(35,40,44,49) sts.
Next Row: P to last 6 sts, [K1, P1] 3 times.
Next Row: [K1, P1] 3 times, K to end.
Rep last 2 rows until front meas same as back to shoulder, ending with a RS row.

Shape shoulder and back neck band
Next row: Cast off 25(29,34,38,43), rib to end. 6 sts.
Cont in rib until band reaches halfway round back neck when slightly stretched, ending with WS row.
Cast off in rib.

SLEEVES (both alike)
Using 3¼mm needles and yarn A cast on 44(46,48,50,52) sts.
Row 1: * K1, P1, rep from * to end.
Row 1 forms rib.
Cont in rib until work meas 12cm, ending with a WS row.

Change to 4mm needles.
Working stripe patt as given for back throughout, cont as follows
Work 6 rows.
Next Row (RS): K2, M1, K to last 2 sts, M1, K2.
Work 5 rows.
Working increases as set above, inc 1 st at each end of next and every foll 6th row to 72(74,76,80,84) sts.
Cont without shaping until sleeve meas 47(47,48,48,49) cm, ending with a WS row.

Shape top
Cast off 4 sts at beg of next 2 rows. 64(66,68,72,76) sts.
Next Row: K2, Sl 1, K1, psso, K to last 4 sts, K2tog, K2.
Next Row: P2, P2tog, P to last 4 sts, P2tog tbl, P2. 60(62,64,68,72) sts.
Next Row: K2, Sl 1, K1, psso, K to last 4 sts, K2tog, K2.
Next Row: P to end.
Rep last 2 rows, 3 times more. 52(54,56,60,64) sts.
Cast off.

MAKING UP
Press as described on the information page.
Join both shoulder seams using mattress stitch.
Join cast off edges of back neck bands together, then sew band to back neck.
Sew in sleeves.
Join side and sleeve seams.

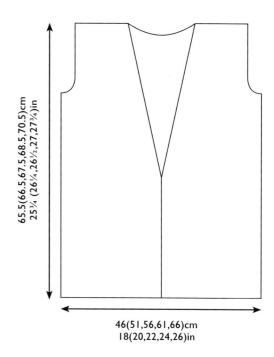

65.5(66.5,67.5,68.5,70.5)cm
25¾ (26¼,26½,27,27¾)in

46(51,56,61,66)cm
18(20,22,24,26)in

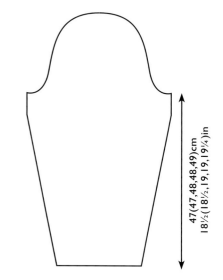

47(47,48,48,49)cm
18½(18½,19,19,19¼)in

SLIP
quail studio

SIZES

To fit bust	81 – 86	91 – 97	102 – 107	112 – 117	122 – 127	cm
	32 – 34	36 – 38	40 – 42	44 – 46	48 – 50	in
Actual Size	87	97	106	116	126	cm
	34¼	38¼	41¾	45½	49½	in

YARN

Rowan Summerlite DK (photographed in Sailor Blue 470)

	4	5	5	6	6	x 50gm

NEEDLES

2¾mm (no 12) (US 2) needles

TENSION

25 sts and 35 rows to 10cm/4in measured over rib when slightly stretched using 2¾mm (US 2) needles

EXTRAS

Stitch Holder

BACK
Using 2¾mm (US 2) needles cast on
109(121,133,145,157) sts.
Row 1 (RS): K1, * P1, K1, rep from * to end.
Row 2: P1, * K1, P1, rep from * to end.
Rows 1 and 2 form rib.

Cont in rib until back meas 33(34,35,36,37) cm, ending with a WS row.

Shape armholes

Cast off 4 sts at beg of next 2 rows.
101(113,125,137,149) sts.

Next Row: P2tog, rib to last 2 sts, P2tog tbl.
Next Row: P2tog tbl, rib to last 2 sts, P2tog.
Next Row: P2tog, rib to last 2 sts, P2tog tbl.
95(107,119,131,143) sts.

Cont without shaping until armhole meas 19(20,21,22,23) cm, ending with a WS row.

Shape shoulders

Cast off 6(7,9,10,11) sts at beg of next 6 rows and 6(8,8,10,12) sts at beg of foll 2 rows. 47(49,49,51,53) sts. Leave rem sts on a stitch holder.

FRONT
Using 2¾mm (US 2) needles cast on
109(121,133,145,157) sts.
Row 1 (RS): K1, * P1, K1, rep from * to end.
Row 2: P1, * K1, P1, rep from * to end.
Rows 1 and 2 form rib.

Cont in rib until front meas 33(34,35,36,37) cm, ending with a WS row.

Shape armhole and neck

Next Row (RS): Cast off 4, rib until there are 48(54,60,66,72) sts on right hand needle, skpo, turn and work on these 49(55,61,67,73) sts only.

Next Row: Rib to end.
Next Row: P2tog, rib to last 2 sts, P2tog tbl.
Next Row: Rib to last 2 sts, P2tog.
Next Row: P2tog, rib to last 2 sts, skpo.
44(50,56,62,68) sts.
Next Row: Rib to end.
Next Row: Rib to last 2 sts, P2tog tbl.
Next Row: Rib to end.
Next Row: Rib to last 2 sts, skpo.

Working decs as set above, cont to dec 1 st at neck edge on every foll alt row to 24(29,35,40,45) sts.

Cont without shaping until front matches length of back to start of shoulder shaping, ending with a WS row.

Shape shoulder
Cast off 6(7,9,10,11) sts at beg of next row and foll 2 alt rows. 6(8,8,10,12) sts.
Rib 1 row.
Cast off.

With RS facing, sl centre st onto stitch holder, rejoin yarn to rem sts and K2tog, rib to end. 53(59,65,71,77) sts.
Next Row: Cast off 4, rib to end. 49(55,61,67,73) sts.
Next Row: P2tog, rib to last 2 sts, P2tog tbl.
Next Row: P2tog tbl, rib to end.
Next Row: K2tog, rib to last 2 sts, P2tog tbl.
44(50,56,62,68) sts.
Next Row: Rib to end.
Next Row: P2tog, rib to end.
Next Row: Rib to end.
Next Row: K2tog, rib to end.

Working decs as set above, cont to dec 1 st at neck edge on every foll alt row to 24(29,35,40,45) sts.

Cont without shaping until front matches length of back to start of shoulder shaping, ending with a RS row.

Shape shoulder
Cast off 6(7,9,10,11) sts at beg of next row and foll 2 alt rows. 6(8,8,10,12) sts.
Rib 1 row.
Cast off.

MAKING UP
Press as described on the information page.
Join right shoulder seam using mattress stitch.
Neck edging
With RS facing and using 2¾mm (US 2) needles, pick up and knit 58(62,66,70,74) sts down left front neck, K1 st from centre front, pick up and knit 58(62,66,70,74) sts up right front neck, knit 47(49,49,51,53) sts from back neck stitch holder. 164(174,182,192,202) sts.
Cast off, working 3 sts tog at centre of front neck.
Join left shoulder and neck edging seam.
Armhole edging – both alike
With RS facing and using 2¾mm (US 2) needles, pick up and knit 116(124,132,140,148) sts evenly around armhole edge.
Cast off.

Join side and armhole edging seams.

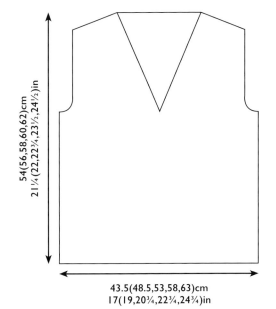

54(56,58,60,62)cm
21¼(22,22¾,23½,24½)in

43.5(48.5,53,58,63)cm
17(19,20¾,22¾,24¾)in

INFORMATION

TENSION

Obtaining the correct tension is perhaps the single factor which can make the difference between a successful garment and a disastrous one. It controls both the shape and size of an article, so any variation, however slight, can distort the finished garment. Different designers feature in our books and it is their tension, given at the start of each pattern, which you must match. We recommend that you knit a square in pattern and/or stocking stitch (depending on the pattern instructions) of perhaps 5 - 10 more stitches and 5 - 10 more rows than those given in the tension note. Mark out the central 10cm square with pins. If you have too many stitches to 10cm try again using thicker needles, if you have too few stitches to 10cm try again using finer needles. Once you have achieved the correct tension your garment will be knitted to the measurements indicated in the size diagram shown at the end of the pattern.

After working for hours knitting a garment, it seems a great pity that many garments are spoiled because such little care is taken in the pressing and finishing process. Follow the text below for a truly professional-looking garment.

Block out each piece of knitting and following the instructions on the ball band press the garment pieces, omitting the ribs. Tip: Take special care to press the edges, as this will make sewing up both easier and neater. If the ball band indicates that the fabric is not to be pressed, then covering the blocked out fabric with a damp white cotton cloth and leaving it to stand will have the desired effect. Darn in all ends neatly along the selvage edge or a colour join, as appropriate.

STITCHING

When stitching the pieces together, remember to match areas of colour and texture very carefully where they meet. Use a seam stitch such as back stitch or mattress stitch for all main knitting seams and join all ribs and neckband with mattress stitch, unless otherwise stated.

CONSTRUCTION

Having completed the pattern instructions, join left shoulder and neckband seams as detailed above. Sew the top of the sleeve to the body of the garment using the method detailed in the pattern, referring to the appropriate guide:

Straight cast-off sleeves: Place centre of cast-off edge of sleeve to shoulder seam. Sew top of sleeve to body, using markers as guidelines where applicable.

Square set-in sleeves: Place centre of cast-off edge of sleeve to shoulder seam. Set sleeve head into armhole, the straight sides at top of sleeve to form a neat right-angle to cast-off sts at armhole on back and front.

Shallow set-in sleeves: Place centre of cast off edge of sleeve to shoulder seam. Match decreases at beg of armhole shaping to decreases at top of sleeve. Sew sleeve head into armhole, easing in shapings.

Set-in sleeves: Place centre of cast-off edge of sleeve to shoulder seam. Set in sleeve, easing sleeve head into armhole. Join side and sleeve seams.
Slip stitch pocket edgings and linings into place.
Sew on buttons to correspond with buttonholes.
Ribbed welts and neckbands and any areas of garter stitch should not be pressed.

ABBREVIATIONS

K	knit
P	purl
st(s)	stitch(es)
inc	increas(e)(ing)
dec	decreas(e)(ing)
st st	stocking stitch (1 row K, 1 row P)
g st	garter stitch (K every row)
beg	begin(ning)
foll	following
rem	remain(ing)
rev st st	reverse stocking stitch (1 row K , 1 row P)
rep	repeat
alt	alternate
cont	continue
patt	pattern
tog	together
mm	millimetres
cm	centimetres
in(s)	inch(es)
RS	right side
WS	wrong side
sl 1	slip one stitch
psso	pass slipped stitch over
p2sso	pass 2 slipped stitches over
tbl	through back of loop
M1	make one stitch by picking up horizontal loop before next stitch and knitting into back of it
M1P	make one stitch by picking up horizontal loop before next stitch and purling into back of it
yfwd	yarn forward
yrn	yarn round needle
meas	measures
0	no stitches, times or rows
-	no stitches, times or rows for that size
yo	yarn over needle
yfrn	yarn forward round needle
wyib	with yarn at back
sl2togK	slip 2 stitches together knitways

MACHINE WASH SYMBOLS

HAND WASH SYMBOLS

DRY CLEAN SYMBOLS

IRONING SYMBOLS

DO NOT BLEACH SYMBOL

DRYING SYMBOLS